NARRATING OUR NATIONS

Teape Lectures 1996-97

Delivered by
ROGER T. HOOKER

Edited by
F. J. BALASUNDARAM

Published by
**the I.S.P.C.K. for
United Theological College,
Bangalore, 1998**

Published jointly for United Theological College, Post Box 4613, 63 Miller Road, Bangalore-560046 by the Indian Society for Promoting Christian Knowledge, Post Box 1585, Kashmere Gate, Delhi–110006 by Rev. Ashish Amos.

BR
128
.H5
H667
1998

ISBN: 81-7214-435-0

Laser typeset and cover design by ISPCK, Post Box 1585, 1654, Madarsa Road, Kashmere Gate, Delhi–110006, Phone: 2966323, Fax: 91-11-2965490

Printed at Cambridge Press, Kashmere Gate, Delhi.

CONTENTS

CONTENTS

From the Editor

What is the use of novels ? Is there any use going through them? These Questions will evoke different responses. Such responses could include expressions or remarks such as "it is a waste of time", "What is there to learn?" etc.

But the author of this book, Revd. Canon Dr. Roger T. Hooker, comes out with an unusual but a brilliant response. According to him novels offer a fruitful way into making sense of our plural world. He makes the point that through novels conversations are made, that they enable us to over-hear conversations which are already going on and, that they offer a new depth and complexity to inter-faith conversation and dialogue. Most importantly, they raise many questions about religion and therefore, novels are important for religious people.

Novels narrate stories, individual as well as collective. In and through them, we learn the voices of the victims and these victims challenge us to reshape our accounts of our own identity. In other words, novels help us to "narrate our nations". Dr. Hooker examines in this book three novels and clearly shows that novelists can be our allies in this struggle.

As a co-organiser, with Mr. Jyothi Sahi, I had the privilege to listen to the three lectures delivered by Dr. Hooker, and like many who had attended the lecture, I was quite impressed by his insights and learnt a lot from his presentations. In bringing out this book, we, the UTCians,

hope that readers would be helped to redefine their identities and reshape their worldview to become more inclusive, rather than being arrogant, blind and exclusive.

On behalf of United Theological College, I thank
Dr. Hooker for enabling us to bring out this work and we
also thank the Teape Lecture Committee. As a co-organiser
I thank Dr. Jyothi Sahi and Dr. David. C. Scott who helped
in the organisation of the Teape lecture at UTC. I thank
also Dr. Gnana Robinson, Principal, UTC, Dr. O.V.
Jathanna, Director of Research and Post-Graduate Studies
and Dr. David. C. Scott, Professor of Religion at the UTC
for kindly consenting to moderate the Lecture sessions.
I also thank Dr. D. Jones Muthunayagom, Convenor, UTC
Publications Committee, for helping us to process the material to the press and the I.S.P.C.K. for publishing this
book for the UTC.

F. J. Balasundaram

October, 1997   Editor

Director of Research and
Post-Graduate Studies, UTC

Acknowledgements

The Teape Lectureship exists because of the generous provision for its establishment which William Teape made in his will. He was born in 1862 and was a student at St. John's College, Cambridge in the 1880s where he came under the influence of the great Bishop Westcott. Westcott was one of the pioneers of the modern critical study of the Bible. He also had an abiding interest in India where several of his sons served as missionaries. This was no narrowly academic concern, for Westcott was a key figure in the founding of the Cambridge Mission to Delhi (now the Brotherhood of the Ascended Christ), one of the aims of which was the promotion of what we would to-day call dialogue between Hindus and Christians. That concern may well have been reflected in the lectures which the young William Teape heard Westcott deliver. After gaining his degree at Cambridge, Teape was ordained as a priest into the Church of England and served as a curate in Durham in the north east of the country. Later, he went to Australia and on his return journey visited India, staying with two of Bishop Westcott's sons in Kanpur. This aroused the interest in things Indian which Westcott senior had perhaps sparked off in the first place. After his return from India he went back to the Diocese of Durham and was Curate of the Parish Church, Stockton-on-Tees. Co-incidentally, I was also Curate of this church from 1960 to 1963.

In his will Teape stipulated that the Lectures should be about 'The Upanishads in the Catholic Church', and he also named three books on Indian philosophy with which he expected the Lecturer to be acquainted. As is the way of most Lectureships, the original terms proved to be too constricting in the light of experience. They were quickly broadened to cover any aspect of Hindu-Christian encounter and dialogue. Teape died in 1944, and the first lecturer, in 1955, was Charles Raven. Since that date the Lectures have alternated each year between England and India.

This book is based on the three Teape Lectures which I delivered at three centres in India during November and December 1996. Two of these centres were the United Theological College, Bangalore and St. Stephen's College, Delhi. The third centre was the Henry Martyn Institute for Islamic Studies, Hyderabad, whose Director arranged for the first Lecture to be delivered at the Sarojini Naidu Institute for the Performing Arts, and the second at The JN Institute of Management and Entrepreneurship. The third was at the Henry Martyn Institute itself. I also delivered a single Lecture, which summarised the contents of the complete set, at Bharat Kala Bhavan, Banaras Hindu University, Varanasi.

I wish to place on record my gratitude to the staff and other members of these institutions for the warm welcome and generous hospitality which they extended to my wife and myself. I am also especially grateful to all who attended the Lectures, both members of these centres and their guests. Their questions and critical comments have played an important part in helping me to re-shape my original text, though of course the final responsibility for what I have written is mine alone.

Last, but certainly not least I want to place on record my particular gratitude to those who gave much time and effort to organising the Lectures, especially to Dr. Gnana

Robinson, Principal of UTC, Bangalore, to his colleague Dr. Franklyn. J. Balasundaram, and to Dr. Jyoti Sahi. I am particularly grateful to Dr. Robinson and Dr. Balasundaram for kindly offering to publish the Lectures. I also want to thank others who organised the Lectures in other venues: Professor George Michael and Mrs. D'Souza of HMI, Hyderabad; Dr. Horace Jacob, Acting Principal of St. Stephen's College Delhi, and his colleagues; and Dr. Bettina Baumer and also to Professor Sharma, Director of the Bharat Kala Bhavan of Banaras Hindu University.

The Excerpts from *The Feuding Families of Village Gangauli* by Rahi Masoom Reza, translated from the Hindi by Gillian Wright, are reproduced courtesy of Mrs Nayyar Reza and the publishers (Penguin Books India Pvt. Ltd.).

Roger Hooker

1997

Introduction

In many parts of the world to-day communities are redefining and asserting their identity in narrow and exclusive religious terms. This threatens the unity and cohesion of states and brings religion and politics together in a dangerous way. In the chapters that follow I explore this situation in the light of three modern Hindi novels. By reading the novels in the light of Christian theological perspectives we can both illuminate this issue in new and potentially fruitful ways, and at the same time discern in the novels an important message beyond their original context and readership.

In the first chapter I suggest that before the coming of mass literacy and the rise of the modern nation state most communities found their identity and made sense of their lives within the framework of a single over-arching sacred narrative or 'epic'– the Bible in Europe, the story of Rama in much of North India. With the coming of the modern world and the massive changes which it has brought, many people found that the framework provided by such traditional narratives were no longer adequate to contain and interpret their new experience. Therefore they constructed new narratives through which to explore and define their identity. Among these were the novel. In the Indian context a novel which describes the passing of the old world of 'epic' is Rahi Masoom Reza's *Half the*

Village.[1] This describes a Shi'i Muslim community whose life was built around the keeping of Moharrum, an inclusive festival in which anyone could join. Reza shows how this community disintegrated at the time of Partition because in the end it was powerless to withstand those who spoke an exclusive language, either Hindu or Muslim.

While Reza describes a community whose members were only aware of themselves as members of a traditional society, in *Shekhar: a Life*[2], S H Vatsyayan 'Ajneya' tells the story of a young man who made the painful journey to self-discovery of himself as an individual person. At the beginning of this novel Shekhar is under sentence of death for having taken part in revolutionary violence against the British, and finds himself compelled to write the story of his life in order to make sense of it. He is fiercely critical of his own Brahminical Hindu inheritance.

He redefines the transcendental and social boundaries within which human life is understood as being lived. He has a passionate social conscience and campaigns on behalf of women and of the poor. These are concerns which Christians should share. At the same time, because Shekhar has stepped outside the boundaries of traditional 'epic vision' it is possible for Christians who have done the same thing to engage him in conversation in a way which we would not easily have done with the characters of *Half*

---

[1]Rahi Masoom Reza, *Adha Gamv*, Rajkamal Prakashan, New Delhi and Patna, 1966. There is an English translation of this novel, for details of which see Chapter One, note 9.

[2]'Ajneya,' *Shekhar: Ek Jivani*, Saraswati Press, Allahabad and Delhi, two volumes 1941 and 1944. This novel has not been translated into English.

the Village. Like Shekhar, we too can and must look at our tradition with critical eyes, even though in some respects our conclusions will not be the same as his. While this novel does not directly 'narrate the nation' in the way that *Half the Village* does, I argue that we can only narrate our nations to-day if we take into account the many people whose struggles and whose perspective on life is reflected in *Shekhar: a Life.*

Communities which define their identity in religious terms to-day often perceive themselves as victims — as deprived of their rights and opportunities by other groups which they see as being in competition with, and more powerful than themselves. This makes for fragmentation and conflict, yet there is a positive way of understanding the status of victim, as is shown by Yashpal's novel, *A False Truth.*[3] Yashpal tells the story of those whom he sees as the victims of the upheavals of Partition in 1947— mainly Punjabi refugees, Communists, and women — and so challenges the dominant version of the events of that period in which the key roles are played by Gandhi, Nehru and the Congress Party. His novel illustrates one way of listening to the stories of the victims. I argue that to do this in our present context we need the kind of maturity and self-awareness which all religions have at their best made available to their followers, but that this needs to be enlarged and informed by the critical perspective of Shekhar. But it is not enough simply for the stories of the victims to be told and heard. The powerful have to modify their own account of who they are in such a way that the stories of

---

[3]Yashpal, *Jhutha Sach*, Viplav Karyalaya, Lucknow, two volumes 1958 and 1960. This novel has not been translated into English.

the victims are included within it. Only so can we narrate
the stories of our different nations in a way which includes
all their citizens.

Although Yashpal writes as an atheist this novel
extends the possibilities of dialogue with Christians which
we have already found to be implicitly present in *Shekhar:
a Life*. The four Gospels can be read as four different
narratives about a victim who in his death was thrust out
beyond the boundaries of society, but who in these four
narratives is the centre of the story.

If the argument of this book carries conviction then it
follows that not only Hindi novels but those written in
other Indian languages could be read in a similar way.
Here is a rich and so far largely untapped resource for
Christian study and research. Furthermore, to engage with
novels in the way in which I have tried to do in these
chapters could open up fruitful possibilities of dialogue
and conversation with their readers.

CHAPTER ONE :
From Epic to the Novel

I begin this first chapter by describing some of my own experiences, not I trust as an exercise in self-indulgence, but because that experience has determined both the subject which I have chosen to address, and the manner in which I have chosen to handle it.

My wife and I first came to India in 1965 under the auspices of what was then called the Church Missionary Society[1], one of the leading Anglican agencies for locating people in churches outside Britain. We arrived with far too much baggage. No-one had told us how little we really needed to bring. That over-loadedness was symbolic. We came encumbered with a number of assumptions which we soon found we had to shed. For example, we had recently married and everyone – not least myself – assumed that my wife should naturally give up her career as a graduate teacher in order to spend her time looking after me and running our home. Put in more general terms that means that in those days women's issues were not part of our common agenda in the way that they are today. My task was to be teaching theology to students who were training to be pastors of village Christian congregations in North India. The assumption that after three years as a young priest in England I could help to teach and to train people

---

[1]Since 1995 The Church Mission Society.

who came from a totally different background and thought-world from my own seems now to be unbelievably naive, not to say arrogant. However, this plan did have one great benefit for which I remain permanently grateful. The medium of instruction in the college at Bareilly for which we were destined was Hindi, and so those who were responsible for us wisely insisted that our first two years in India should be largely devoted to learning it.

I very soon found that I was actually learning not one language but three: first there was the Hindi of my fellow-missionaries. That was easy to understand: we were all thinking in English and translating our thoughts into Hindi as best we could. That is the way in which we all normally begin learning to speak any language which is not our mother tongue. Second was the Hindi, or rather Urdu, of the Christian Church. This was more difficult to grasp, but the Indian Christians shared with the missionaries a common vocabulary based on the Bible. Words like grace, forgiveness, prayer, apostle, parable were all standard. The third language, and the one which I found much the hardest to understand, was the Hindi spoken by Hindus when they were talking about their own tradition. The reasons for this difficulty I describe below. I first became dimly aware of it when I began to meet Hindus, and to read their scriptures and other books. It soon became apparent that for this purpose the Hindi of the Church was much too limited. So after completing the statutory two years course, I decided to continue my studies and do the optional Advanced Course, as it was called.

In the course several texts were prescribed reading. Two of these were to have a profound influence on me, and the impact they made, and indeed continue to make, is central to all that I want to say in this book. The first was part of the *Ramacharitamanas* of Tulsi Das, the great sixteenth century devotional poem of North India, large parts of which many illiterate people in those days knew by heart. One evening in 1969 a Hindu friend invited me to attend a *satsang* at the home of a jeweller in Bareilly. I found myself sitting in the open inner courtyard of the house together with some fifteen other people – members of the family and neighbours. They met in this way every Thursday. They would take it in turns to chant a passage of the *Ramacharitamanas* to a hauntingly beautiful melody. The passage was then expounded by a pundit in Hindi. Afterwards a second pundit would read a short passage from the Gita in Sanskrit and then expound that in Hindi.

I attended this *satsang* regularly for three years and it was my first real encounter with 'Hindu Hindi'. To begin with I found the experience intensely frustrating. By that time I was, I had supposed, making good progress in learning and understanding the language. I was teaching in the theological college and my students seemed to be able to grasp what I was saying. Provided they spoke slowly I could understand them – though I still understood all too little of the mental and spiritual universe in which they lived. In the *satsang,* however, while I could understand most of the words and the grammar, I could make very little sense of what was actually being said. At first I could not understand why this was so, but eventually the reason for my incomprehension dawned on me. What I was failing to pick up was the stories, the allusions, and the assumptions which lay behind what was being said, but which were left unsaid, because everyone present – except me – knew what they were. And so I formulated what for me remains the cardinal first principle of all communication – and therefore of all inter-religious dialogue: I can only understand what another person says if I have first understood what they have left unsaid.

To focus that principle a little more sharply I must continue the story further: after three years at the theological college in Bareilly my family and I moved to Varanasi. There for six years I was a student at the Sanskrit University[2] where I studied Sanskrit through the medium of Hindi, sitting at the feet of traditional pundits. During the festival of Diwali my family and I would sometimes take a boat out on the Ganges, have a picnic supper, and enjoy the firework display, as well as the beautiful sight of the many miniature oil lamps which Hindu devotees floated on to the river in little clay bowls. One year I was unexpectedly given an excellent illustration of my first principle of communication. Knowing that boatmen occupied a low position in the caste hierarchy I asked ours how he was treated by people belonging to the higher castes. 'They treat us very well', he said proudly, 'after all it was we who took Rama across the river.' The grammar and the vocabulary of that sentence were perfectly clear, but what did it actually mean ?

By a happy co-incidence, that very morning I had been reading in the *Ramacharitamanas* the very story to which the boatman was referring. The story was this: during the course of his wanderings in the jungle Rama had touched a rock with his feet. The rock turned into a beautiful woman, Ahalya. She had been put under a curse from which she had been promised that the touch of the great

---

[2]During my time there its name was changed to the Sampurnananda Sanskrit University. It should not be confused with the much larger, better known, and much more westernised Banaras Hindu University.

Rama's feet would release her.[3] Shortly after her release Rama arrived at the Ganges and asked a boatman to ferry him across. The boatman said that since the touch of Rama's feet had turned a rock into a woman, who could say what they would do to his boat, on which his whole livelihood depended ? He would only take Rama across if he would first allow him to wash his feet. Rama agreed to this and all was well.[4] Now when the boatman said to me, 'It was we who took Rama across the river', he assumed that all that I have just written was already in my mind, as of course it was in his. After all, how could anyone not know who the great Rama was, and not know this story ? No doubt it was particularly in his mind on that evening, for one of the great stories associated with Diwali is of course the return of Rama in triumph to the city of Ayodhya from which he had been exiled fourteen years previously.

Notice that the boatman was not, as it were, looking back to the Epic of Rama as something belonging to a remote past. He did not feel that this was an ancient text which was separated from his own time by the passing of the centuries. He had no need of a commentary to bridge the gap between then and now. We can almost say that he was speaking from within the Epic. It was the mental world which he inhabited and that story about Rama defined his identity. In the most profound sense he was at home within the text – or rather within the story – because he was almost certainly illiterate. Further, his identity was collective: it was shared by other boatmen. 'It was we who took

---

[3]*Bala Kanda* 1.D 210 and Ch 22. For an English translation of this passage see W D P Hill, *The Holy Lake of the Acts of Rama,* OUP India, 1952, p 97.
[4]*Ayodhya Kanda* Ch 100, Hill, 1952, p 202.

Rama across the river.' Finally, it was a narrative identity,
it was created by the story.

Nor of course was this only true of boatmen. Towards
the end of my six years in Varanasi I decided to write a
book in which I planned to get a number of my Hindu
friends to tell their own personal stories. This project proved
far more difficult than I had thought it would be, and
eventually I had to abandon it and plan the book on different lines. I asked one of my Sanskrit teachers if he would
tell me his story, but he replied: 'What is there to say ? I
am just an ordinary pundit'. In other words, 'My identity
is defined by my role and my role is given to me by tradition'. The very idea of himself as a unique and distinctive
person with a life-story which made him different from
other persons was not something he could comprehend. My
problem was that I was assuming that the western ideal of
the self-conscious independent individual was in fact universal. This was another piece of mental and cultural baggage which I had brought with me to India and which I had
to shed.

Now the boatman and the pundit are simply examples
of a much wider phenomenon. A Christian version of it is
described by Hans Frei. In 1974 he published an important
and very influential book called *The Eclipse of Biblical
Narrative*.[5] In it he points out that in mediaeval Britain, as
in most of the old Christendom, it was the Bible, understood as a single over-arching narrative from Genesis to
Revelation, which provided the framework within which
all human life was understood and interpreted. He writes:

Since the world truly rendered by combining biblical

---

[5]H Frei, *The Eclipse of Biblical Narrative*, Yale University
Press, New Haven and London, 1974.

narratives into one was indeed the one and only real world it must in principle embrace the experience of any age and reader. Not only was it possible for him, it was also his duty to fit himself into that world in which in any case he was a member. (Frei 1974 p3).

Frei argues that in the eighteenth century that framework began to break down. It could no longer contain the new experiences and new forms of life which were emerging — at least in the lives of the new middle classes. To quote him again:

[There followed][6] a gradual change to the sense of another temporal reality than the biblical. The self might or might not claim this new historical world as its appropriate home, but in any case the true narrative by which its reality is rendered is no longer identical with the Bible's over-arching story. (Frei 1974 p 50).

Since the Bible could no longer fulfil its traditional role, other kinds of narrative emerged and were used to make sense of peoples' lives. Among these was the novel. In other words, it is only possible to write and to read novels when that old unitary world is fractured. A very similar process happened in India, only much later and on a smaller scale. In the Hindi language area the first novelist whom we can call genuinely modern in that he does not simply provide romantic diversion and entertainment, was Prem Chand, who died in 1936. Here I must briefly retrace my steps: I wrote above that in that advanced Hindi course which I studied back in the sixties there were two

---

[6]Square brackets within a quotation, as here, indicate that I have added the words within them in order to make the meaning of the passage clear.

texts in particular which made a considerable impact on
me. The first was the *Ramacharitamanas*, which I have
already discussed. The second was Prem Chand's classic
novel *Godan, The Gift of a Cow*. This book describes the
struggles of a villager called Hori against caste discrimination, against unscrupulous money lenders, against the
climate, and against other members of his own family.
Hori is always struggling to maintain his *dharma*, but can
never manage to do so.[7] *Godan* was the first novel to open
up the world of village India to a wider public. The reading
of it led me to read many other Hindi novels. It is about
three of them and about some of the issues which they raise
that I write in these chapters. These issues are universal
and should be of importance to all thoughtful and responsible people in 1997.

The novel as a literary *genre* readily lends itself to
this kind of use, for one of its characteristics is that it
travels remarkably well. You do not have to be a nineteenth century Russian, or someone who is interested in
nineteenth century Russian history and literature, in order
to appreciate *The Brothers Karamazov or War and Peace*.
These novels speak to us all. Again one does not need to
know the life of Malgudi, or its South Indian equivalent, at
first hand, in order to enjoy and appreciate the novels of R
K Narayan. Nor do you have to be English in order to
understand the novels of Thomas Hardy. Indeed it has been
suggested that Hardy's Wessex novels can serve as broadly
accurate descriptions of Punjabi village life fifty years

---

[7]I owe this insight to a comment by the Hindi writer Nirmala
Varma, who made it while chairing one of the Lectures on
which this book is based, at St. Stephen's College, Delhi.

ago.[8] Again, the novels of the Nigerian Chinua Achebe are
widely read in India.[9] Nor is this all: among the most
famous of English nineteenth century novelists are the
Bronte sisters, Anne, Charlotte and Emily. Their home in
the North of England, Haworth Parsonage, is kept as a
museum dedicated to their memory. The signs to guide
visitors around the house are now in two languages: one of
course is English, but the other is Japanese. Emily Bronte's
novel *Wuthering Heights* speaks profoundly to the Japanese soul. So Japanese tourists in their hundreds flock to
Haworth Parsonage as to a place of pilgrimage. The person
who told me this was a white English monk of the
Ramakrishna Mission! He suggested that we shall only
really understand *Wuthering Heights* when someone interprets it in terms of *Samkhya* philosophy. That suggestion
gives me confidence as a British Christian in presuming to
attempt to say something new about novels written in an
Indian language. Great novels, the classics, can speak to
people of any time and of any place. Lesser ones, of the
kind which I shall be discussing in these chapters, may not
travel so well, or last so long, but they can still illuminate
contemporary issues, enable us to see the world through
new eyes, and so open up new possibilities of living. And
in new situations all novels can yield new interpretations
of which their authors were not aware.

---

[8]A Sikh friend of mine in Birmingham, England, made this
point to me in conversation in 1989.

[9]Professor Harish Trivedi, Professor of English Literature in
the University of Delhi, told me in a conversation in 1991
that many of his students find that Achebe's novels speak to
them in their own struggles to find a post-colonial identity.

The novel as a literary form functions very differently from the *Ramacharitamanas* or the Bible, or the Qur'an, or indeed from any other overarching text which defines, or used to define, the life of a whole society. To hear the Bible read in church, to join in a *satsang* where the *Ramacharitamanas* is recited, to listen to the recitation of the whole of the Qur'an during the fast of Ramadan – these are essentially corporate experiences. They bind together those who live in the world which is shaped and defined by the text concerned. To read a novel on the other hand, you have to be literate, and the reading is a solitary experience, which separates those who have had it from those who have not. Also of course, a novel is a different kind of text. That difference is well-expressed in some words of Carlos da Fuentes, a Latin American writer who wrote them in an article in an English newspaper at the time of the Rushdie affair in March 1989:

> When we all understood everything, the epic was possible, but not fiction. The novel is born from the fact that we do not understand one another any longer, because unitary orthodox language has broken down. Quixote and Sancho, the Shandy brothers, Mr and Mrs Karenin: their novels are the comedy (or the drama) of their misunderstandings. Impose a unitary language: you kill the novel, but you also kill the society. (The Guardian Weekly, 5th March 1989, pp 8-9).

Fuentes implicitly endorses my claim that the novel travels easily: Quixote and Sancho are of course the two main characters of Cervantes' novel *Don Quixote* which he wrote in fifteenth century Spain. The Shandy brothers feature in *Tristram Shandy* which Laurence Sterne wrote in eigh-

teenth century England, while Mr and Mrs Karenin are two
of the main characters in *Anna Karenin* which Tolstoy
wrote in nineteenth century Russia.

But to return to the words of Fuentes, part of the great
crisis of our time is that there are those in all cultures who
are trying to impose their own unitary languages, and unitary view of the world, on everyone else. My claim is that
a study of the novel as a literary form, and of some novels
in particular, can help us to understand a little better just
why they are doing this, and also help us to work out what
I want to call 'a strategy of resistance'. Notice Fuentes'
striking phrase 'When we all understood everything'. Of
course we never did, but the point is we or our forebears
thought we did, because we knew little or nothing beyond
the parameters of our own societies. To understand everything is to be at home, and it is also to be in control. To
lose one's home and to lose control is a very disturbing
experience. It is to be an exile, and to a degree we are all
exiles today.

Fuentes goes on:

Fiction is a harbinger of a multi-polar and multicultural
world, where no single philosophy, no single belief,
no single solution, can thrust aside the extreme wealth
of mankind's cultural heritage. Our future depends on
the enlarged freedom for the multicultural and
polycultural to express itself in a world of shifting,
decaying and emerging power centres.

The novel, therefore, is at one level, about the meeting of
different world-views. That meeting does not always lead
to mutual understanding, though it can do. Often it is simply about the clash of two individuals, two groups, or two
worlds in mutual incomprehension, but if we the readers,

reflect on the nature and the causes of that clash and of
that incomprehension, then perhaps we can begin to over-
come it in our own lives, and so make a small contribution
to the creation of a more civilised, harmonious, and mutu-
ally comprehending society.

I now illustrate this from the first of my three novels,
Rahi Masoom Reza's *Half the Village*.[10] Reza was a Shi'i
Muslim by origin and a Marxist by conviction. This was
the first novel written in Hindi by an Indian Shi'i about his
own people. He describes the life of a Shi'i village community in the period just before and after independence and
Partition in 1947. The village is called Gangauli and it is
on the north bank of the Ganges about a hundred and ten
kilometres north east of Varanasi. Reza wrote in the
Devanagari script of the Hindi language in order to address
Hindus, and partly no doubt simply to gain a wider readership. He assumes that there will be elements of the life
of the Shi'i Muslim community which will be strange to
Hindu readers. He has an intriguing series of footnotes
which explain various aspects of Shi'i belief and practice
for the benefit of these readers.[11] For example, he explains
that Shi'i women commonly remove their bangles during

---

[10]There is an English translation by Gillian Wright with the
title *The Feuding Families of Village Gangauli*, Viking,
Penguin Books India (P) Ltd., New Delhi, 1994. This title
is somewhat misleading as it focusses our attention on the
internal life of the Shi'i community, which is indeed a
major pre-occupation of the novel, but rather misses the
nuance of Reza's own title. The other half of the village is
where the Hindus live.

[11]In the English translation the footnotes are included in the
text itself, so we lose the important point that the novel is
actually addressed to Hindus.

Moharram as part of their traditional mourning for the
martyr Husain. (H p 40, E p 30)[12] He does not need to
explain to his Hindu readers the obvious parallel to Hindu
mourning customs, where of course a wife breaks her
bangles when her husband dies.

Within this novel there are two kinds of unitary, over-
arching, and all embracing language. The first I call inclusive and the second exclusive. It is the exclusive kind to
which Fuentes refers in the above quotation. This is an
imposed language of exclusive religious orthodoxy which
deliberately allows no alternative to its own claims. In this
novel, as we shall see, this kind of language is always
spoken by people who come from outside the village community. But there is another kind of unitary language which
has a much more positive significance. This is the language spoken within the village community in which people
understand themselves as belonging to the village and not
as Hindus or Muslims. What this excludes is the language
of exclusive religious orthodoxy spoken by the outsiders.
It excludes not deliberately but unconsciously, because
those who speak it find the language which the outsiders
speak literally unintelligible.

Such inclusive unitary language is spoken by the Shi'i
villagers of Gangauli. The over-arching narrative which
interprets the whole of their life and experience — their
equivalent of the *Ramacharitamanas* or the Bible — is the
story of the martyrdom of Husain which is remembered
every year during the ten days of Moharram. Practically
the whole year is spent in preparation for these ten days.

---

[12]In this and in subsequent references 'H' refers to the page
number in the Hindi edition of the novel, and 'E' to that in
the English translation by G Wright.

Moharram is the source of the villagers' philosophy of life
and of their moral values. Within its compass the whole of
their life and the whole of their experience are contained
and interpreted. But Reza is at pains to point out that
Moharram is not exclusive to the Shi'is. Within the village
all sorts of other people can and do join in the keeping of
it. For example, several of the Shi'i men have scheduled
caste Hindu concubines. One of these men is Sulaiman
whose concubine is Jhangtiya-bo.

She

> Could not sit on the floor-covering with the ladies of
> the family, although she was allowed to attend the
> majlises of Moharram. This was because she had a
> very fine voice...

> She didn't become a Muslim, and nor did Sulaiman-
> cha make any attempt to convert her. (H p 42, E p 32).

People of higher castes can also join in. Every year, on the
tenth day of the commemoration of the martyrdom of Husain,
the Great Tazia was taken in procession through the village. A group of men belonging to the Hindu Ahir caste
went in front carrying *lathis*. The Ahirs' task was to poke
down any over-hanging eaves from houses on the route, for
these might impede the stately course of the Tazia — an
insult which could never be allowed.

> One year it so happened that due to a builder's error
> the eaves on the house of a Brahmin widow jutted out
> [over the narrow lane] a little less than they should
> have done. The Great Tazia went by without them
> being knocked down. The widow began to sob, saying
> that the Imam Sahib was angry with her, and so some
> disaster was bound to befall her, otherwise it was
> impossible for the Great Tazia to go by without knock-

ing down her eaves. She took both her sons with her
to the tomb of Nuruddin the Martyr.[13] Then she looked
straight into the unseeing eyes of the Great Tazia and
said, 'Oh Imam Sahib ! If anything happens to my two
boys, it will not be well.' (H p 75, E p 63).

This passage illustrates the way in which the author uses
irony as a device to unite his two conflicting points of
view: Reza the Shi'i demonstrates that a Brahmin woman
can join in Moharram and pray at the tomb of a Muslim
saint, while at the same time Reza the Marxist implicitly
invites his readers to join with him in smiling at her naive
and simplistic faith, and the ridiculous lengths to which
she carries it.

Not only Hindus but also Sunni Muslims can be included in Shi'i celebration. Reza writes:

> Once it was decided to hold the Bismillah ceremony
> of my eldest sister's son on the third day of the month
> *Shaabaan* — Imam Husain's birthday. Accordingly our
> own poets were put aside and it was decided to call
> Khalu Miyan, more properly known as Maulvi Ibne
> Hasan Naunharavi — from Lucknow.

> Khalu Miyan agreed. Now, in the first place this cer-
> emony was being held at our house, and in the second,
> Maulvi Ibne Hasan Naunharavi was going to address
> it, and so there was a large gathering. First Qais
> Jangipuri read a panegyric in praise of Imam Husain
> in which there were many offensive remarks about the
> first three Caliphs accepted and revered by Sunni
> Muslims. A lot of Sunnis had also come to hear the

---

[13]This was a tomb outside the village where the great procession came to its end.

chaste Urdu of the Maulvi, and naturally Father and
other members of the family felt extremely uncom-
fortable. All the educated Sunnis began to fidget.
Anyway, somehow or other they endured the panegy-
ric...

Khalu Miyan stood up. He'd guessed the mood of the
audience. He climbed the pulpit, adjusted the hem of
his coat, very carefully spat out his betel-nut into a
small inlaid metal spittoon placed on its steps, looked
at his pocket watch and recited the verse of the Qur'
an which says poets are misguided and lead others
astray.

The moment the Sunnis heard this, their faces bright-
ened. They sat up happily. (H p 48, E pp 38-9).

As well as the present practice the historical memory
of the Shi'i community can be inclusive of others who were
not Shi'is. The story of Moharram is told in a way which
includes significant Indian references. For example, one of
the Shi'i characters of the novel is called Abbas. He claims
that when on the field of Karbala Imam Husain was invited
to surrender rather than die, he actually told the opposing
general

> 'that if Yazid thought he would rebel he should allow
> him to go to India.'

With an eye to his Hindu readers Reza has Abbas
continue:

> therefore no one who is a follower of Imam Husain
> can wish India ill. After all, the Imam Sahib must
> have had some reason for choosing this land of
> infidels.

Abbas goes on:

> And it's not only that – a Kashmiri Brahmin was also
> martyred at Karbala along with Imam Husain. The
> descendants of that Brahmin call themselves Husaini
> Brahmins. They have a kind of red line around their
> throat like a ribbon. If you don't believe it, take a
> look at Ghazipur's Dr Trilokinath ! He's a Husaini
> Brahmin and he's got that thread of blood on his neck.

> Imam Husain couldn't come to India, but we did. So
> we are not about to leave it now. (H p 61, E p 50).

There we have Reza's main purpose in writing. He is trying to show that the Shi'i Muslims have lived in India for
centuries, and that their community can potentially include
anyone in its major festival. So what right does anyone
have to tell them they must leave and go to Pakistan ?
Behind that is perhaps the implicit suggestion that they
would rather live with a Hindu majority in India than under
Sunni dominance in Pakistan.

We must stand back a little from this novel for a
moment and reflect on the nature of what I have described
as 'inclusive unitary language'. Notice that it is unsophis-
ticated. The characters whom I have quoted do not speak
as self-conscious individual persons. They speak as repre-
sentatives of their community. It is hard to imagine them
telling their own personal stories. If asked to do so they
would no doubt have responded rather like my friend the
pundit in Varanasi, who said, 'I am just an ordinary pundit'.

The world of inclusive unitary language is not only to
be found in the pages of a Reza. He is describing something universal, to be found not only in India wherever
Muslims and Hindus have lived peacefully side by side, as

they have often done for many years, but also, I guess, until recently in a place such as Bosnia, in communities which embraced both Orthodox and Catholic Christians, as well as Muslims. Indeed for me as a European to read this, and the other two novels which I shall be discussing, with Bosnia in mind is to read them with a new sense of humility about our own recent past and about the history which lies behind it. I also read these books with a new sense of their urgency and of their relevance. Nor is this surprising: I have already pointed out that a novel can reveal new depths of meaning when it is read in a new context of which its author knew nothing.

The strength of the kinds of community which Reza describes is also their weakness. They are perilously fragile and vulnerable creations. In the end Gangauli is overwhelmed by forces from outside which its inhabitants can neither understand nor resist. These forces are represented by outsiders who speak the exclusive unitary language of a particular religion. I give two examples of this from Reza's novel. In each case what the outsiders say is unintelligible to the villagers because although in a literal sense they can understand the outsiders' words, each party to the conversation — if we can call it that — is making assumptions which the other does not share. Thus they illustrate my first principle of communication and reflect my experience of that *satsang* in Bareilly. That principle was: I can only understand what another person says if I have first understood what they have left unsaid.

In my first example two Muslim students from the University of Aligarh are visiting Gangauli in order to solicit votes for the Muslim League in the State Assembly elections of 1937. The first person they meet is a young villager called Kammo:

'We hail from Aligarh', said one of the young men in the correct Urdu of an educated city-dweller.

'Eh sahib, are there holidays there nowadays ?'

'No, there are not,' said the second young man, also in Urdu: 'We are not on vacation but you must have heard that elections are at hand.'

'That I have.'

'Your respected mother and father are also voters.'

This sentence intoxicated Kammo. For the first time he had heard his mother called 'respected mother', otherwise she was called neither mother nor wife. She was just Rahman-bo. He smiled.

'Accha, tell me this – will Aligarh go to Pakistan or stay here ?'[14]

'It is our endeavour that Aligarh be incorporated into Pakistan as it is a beacon of Islamic culture.'

'Beacon ?' repeated Kammo in amazement. 'Eh, sahib, I'd heard there was a university there, and you're saying that it's a beacon.'

The young men smiled. They said, 'Please try to see, the reality of the situation is..,'

'Eh sahib, listen here Sahib', interrupted Kammo, 'If Aligarh is to go to Pakistan then say so straight out. Because if it is then my respected mother and father cannot give you their votes !'

'I beg your pardon ?' exclaimed one of the young men.

---

[14]Behind Kammo's question lies the fact that the girl he is in love with has just gone to Aligarh to study.

'If Pakistan is not created then the eighty million
Muslims here will be made, and made to remain
untouchables,' said the other.

'Eh, bhai, it looks to me as if it's been a waste of time
educating you. What else ? If you people don't even
know that Bhangis and Chamars are the untouchables.
What sort of Bhangis and Chamars do you think we
are ? And how can anyone who's not an untouchable
be turned into one, sahib ? Go on, tell me, I'm listening.' (H pp 250-1, E pp 237-8).

And so the conversation continues with a total lack of
communication. In a way the very fact that the villagers
are ignorant of almost anything outside the life of their
own immediate community is a kind of defence, but we, the
readers know that in the end the forces represented by the
two students will prove irresistible.

A very similar kind of exchange takes place between
a Hindu villager from Gangauli and a fanatical Hindu
teacher from a nearby town. The villager is called Chikuriya
and his father has recently been hanged for murder. The
teacher tries to make out that he was a patriotic Hindu
martyr and Reza goes on:

Chikuriya didn't even know that his father had been
killed for undertaking a heroic deed, or that he'd been
martyred. He only knew that Imam Husain had been
martyred, and therefore he believed that to be a martyr you had to be an Imam Sahib. And he also knew
that whatever his father was, he was certainly no Imam
Sahib...

So he said, 'Don't say all these things Master Sahib,
if the Imam hears there'll be hell to pay'.

'Imam Sahib', screamed the sandalwood tika on the
Master Sahib's brow, 'What Imam Sahib ?...Are you
the offspring of an immortal martyr or a Muslim to be
talking such nonsense ?

'Hold on there bhaiyaa, I'm not an idiot. You shouldn't
call the Imam Sahib a Muslim. If he was so, do you
think the Miyans would let us make offerings to him
and that he would accept them ?' (H p 181, E p 169)

So both the Muslim Kammo and the Hindu Chikuriya as-
sume a united village community which includes within it
all who live there, whatever their religion may be. They do
not so much reject, they simply cannot make sense of the
language talked by the outsiders, which defines humanity
in terms of belonging to one religious community to the
exclusion of others. So this novel brings together clashing
world-views, and in doing so it paints a picture of mutual
non-comprehension which to the reader is both comic and
tragic at the same time. We are reminded of the words of
Carlos da Fuentes: the novel is born from the fact that we
do not understand one another any longer.

Half the Village does have a kind of answer to the
problems it describes. Many of the Shi'i villagers do in the
end go to Pakistan. The ones who stay behind lose their
social status. They were *zamindars*, but the *zamindari*
system was abolished in 1952 and so at the end of the book
some of the low caste Hindu villagers now lord it over
their erstwhile Muslim masters, but the village now has
paved *galis*, and there is a tarmac road to connect it to the
nearest town. So Independence brings real material progress.

But we are left with a large question. Gangauli has
gone for ever. Such communities may still survive here and
there, but in the end we know that they are powerless to

resist the encroachments of the outside world in the shape of mass education and the mass media, to say nothing of economic change. Do these influences inevitably create the growth of self-awareness and self-consciousness — the self-consciousness of Reza the novelist as distinct from the characters he describes? Self-awareness means that we can stand outside our own traditions, look at them critically, but can we then still find our identity within the old spiritual home ? Those are the questions I shall be addressing — with the help of another novel — in the next chapter.

CHAPTER TWO :
The Emergence of the Individual

In the previous chapter I briefly described the all-embracing world of epic – using the word epic in the broad sense of an overarching narrative framework within whose parameters a community makes sense of its life. As an example of such a community and such a narrative I took the Shi'i Muslims of Gangauli, as described in Rahi Masoom Reza's novel, *Half the Village*. In that novel the villagers spoke what I described as 'inclusive unitary language', a language which was built around the keeping of Moharram. Anyone who lives in the village can take part in Moharram and many do – the scheduled caste concubine of Sulaiman, who is valued for her fine singing voice, the Brahmin widow who is worried because the eaves of the roof of her house are not knocked down before the passage of the Great Tazia, the local Sunnis who come to hear a speaker who speaks superb Urdu. Their language is unitary in that the villagers are aware of themselves as belonging to a single village community and not as Hindus or Muslims who belong to separate communities which include many other people who live outside the village.

That sense of separateness does govern the perception of outsiders – the two Muslim League students from Aligarh, and the Hindu teacher in the nearby town. These outsiders speak what I described as 'exclusive unitary language'. This is a language which defines identity in terms of

belonging exclusively to one religious community, Hindu
or Muslim. It is a language which the villagers literally
cannot understand, and for the same reasons that I could
not at first understand the language of the *satsang*. They
could understand the words being spoken to them, but they
could not grasp the unspoken assumptions which lay behind them. Instead, they tried to interpret what the outsiders said from within the framework of their own assumptions. Yet in the end it was the external language, and all
that it stood for, which finally overwhelmed them. I con-
trasted the unitary world of epic in which it is possible to
speak only one kind of language, whether inclusive or
exclusive, with the plurality of languages spoken within
the novel as a literary *genre*, and I pointed out that though
western in origin the novel is now universal. Almost every
culture in the world now has its novels and novelists, and
novels travel well. The good ones are translated into many
different languages.

Before moving on to the substance of the present
chapter I draw attention to two points which were implicit
in the previous one, but which I did not spell out. First, the
contrast between what I have described as 'epic vision'
and the novel is not absolute. What unites them is that both
are kinds of stories. All religious traditions have a multi-
tude of stories by means of which their central teachings
are illustrated and handed on down the generations. Within
the Hindu tradition there are plenty of stories to be found
in the Upanishads, and still more in the Epics and Puranas,
while in Christianity we have only to think of the four
Gospels and of the parables of Jesus which they contain.
Stories have always been good travellers. Most English
children of my generation were taught Aesop's Fables in
our infant schools, and these of course had travelled to the
West from India, and no doubt part of the reason why

today novels travel so well is simply that they are stories. Therefore one reason why the novel as a literary form has put down such deep roots in Indian and other cultures is that the soil was already well-prepared in advance. Though genuinely new, the novel was not a totally alien form. If it had been it could not have taken root in the way in which it has.

Second, inter-religious dialogue, to use the current Christian term, is usually thought of as people of different religious traditions listening to and learning from one another – Hindus and Christians in the tradition of the Teape Lectures. Yet, once we start drawing material from novels that simple picture becomes both more complex and richer in possibilities. One feature of the novel is that a conversation – or at least an encounter – is already going on within it, and so the readers are rather like guests who are the privileged listeners to a conversation which other people are having in their presence. Something like that was happening when we as it were 'listened in' to those conversations in Gangauli between the insiders and the outsiders – only of course to call those verbal encounters 'conversations' without further qualification is an over-simplification: the whole point of them is that they were not real conversations for there was no meeting of minds, though we, the readers, could actually understand both parties.

That is an example of the greater complexity and richness to which I have just referred. I believe there are possibilities here for our on-going inter-religious conversation which could profitably be explored further. Another element in our study of *Half the Village* was this: we were not actually present in Gangauli, nor were we actually listening to what was being said there. We were watching and listening through the eyes and ears of the novel's author. Through his use of irony we realised that he was not trying to offer us a straight and literal description. Instead he was standing back from Gangauli and looking at it sympathetically but also critically in a way that none of his characters could do for themselves. I ended the previous chapter by suggesting that this meant that as a writer he was self-aware or self-conscious in a way that was not true of any of his characters. In other words he not only watched and listened, but was aware of himself as watcher and listener. Just what such self-awareness means and what its implications are both for inter-religious conversation and for narrating our nations is the main theme of this second chapter.

In order to explore it I turn to my second novel, *Shekhar: A Life*,[1] by S H Vatsyayan 'Ajneya' (1911 - 1987). This novel is not an autobiography but it does mirror very closely the author's own life and experience. Ajneya's grandfather was a traditional Sanskrit pundit who spent the whole of his life in his home state of the Punjab. His mentality and outlook, and his way of life, will have been very little different from that of the Sanskrit pundits who taught me in Varanasi a century later. Ajneya's father worked for the Archaeological Department of the government of British India and this job took him and his family to many different parts of the country. Much of the first volume of this novel reflects the author's adolescent years which were spent in Ootacamund and Madras. Most of the second volume is set in Lahore and Delhi in the fifteen years before Partition and Independence.

Shortly before he died Ajneya gave an extended radio interview which was broadcast after his death and pub-

---

[1] For publication details, see Introduction, note 2.' This novel has not been translated into English.

lished as a book. In the interview he was asked why he had
not established himself as a writer by writing a long epic
poem based on the Ramayana or Mahabharata as Hindi
writers before him had normally done.[2] His reply to this
question was intriguing:

> In the tradition of those who were writers before me,
> up until Gupta-ji [a well-known Hindi poet of the first
> half of this century] no-one could be called a great
> poet until he had not only written a long poem, but
> one based on a famous story taken from the
> Mahabharata or Ramayana... I do not think that a
> modern epic can be written in that kind of metrical
> verse. The modern 'epic' is the novel.[3]

So here is a modern Indian writer who like many of his
counterparts in the West feels cut off from his inheritance
in that he finds a traditional literary form to be unusable,
and yet at the same time is still engaged with it as he shows
by comparing epic and novel to one another. He almost
claims that novels in general reinterpret tradition. That is
certainly what he does in the novel we shall be considering
in this chapter. What he sets before us is neither an inclusive nor exclusive unitary vision but rather a very personal
and individual one which he invites his readers to share.

The novel begins in melodramatic fashion with the
single word 'Hanging' (*phamsi*). Shekhar is in the con-

---

[2] He was actually best known as a poet and literary critic. He
wrote only three novels, though he set great store by them.

[3] M Lele, R K Maheshwari, and G Gunjan (eds), *Ajneya:
apne bare mem*, Akashvani Prakashan, New Delhi, 1993, p
162. The translation of this, and passages from other Hindi
works for which there is no published English translation,
is my own.

demned cell awaiting execution for the crime of taking part
in revolutionary violence against British rule. He gives us
a series of flashbacks in which he looks back over his past
life. Most of these are later incorporated into the story of
his life which he tells as the novel unfolds. He was born at
an archaeological site in Patna where his father was working. When his father was transferred, the family moved to
Kashmir and then from Kashmir to Ootacamund where the
young Shekhar had an adolescent love affair. This came to
an abrupt and painful end when the girl's family moved
and Shekhar was sent to college in Madras. Then the family moved to Lahore and he went to college there to continue his education. In Lahore he met up again with Shashi,
a young woman whom he had first met when they were
both little children. Shekhar served as a volunteer youth
worker at a Congress Party camp, but like many young
Punjabis of his day, became disillusioned with the
Congress.[4] At the camp he was wrongly arrested and put in
jail. This proved to be a life-transforming experience from
which he emerged determined to write in order to promote
social change and revolution. In this commitment he was
helped and inspired by Shashi. He was drawn into revolutionary activity, arrested and sentenced to death. So he
found himself in jail for a second time, and the novel ends
where it began, in the condemned cell.[5]

---

[4]For the background to this disillusionment see G A Heeger,
'The Growth of the Congress Movement in Punjab 1920-
40', in Journal of Asian Studies, Vol 32 No 1, November
1972. See also K Mohan, *Militant Nationalism in Punjab
1919-1935*, Manohar, New Delhi, 1985.

[5]To say it 'ends' is not strictly accurate. Ajneya always
maintained that he had written a third volume, but this was
never published.

The story is deliberately somewhat disconnected and at times fragmentary. The writer was influenced by contemporary western novelists who had abandoned straight chronological story-telling, of the type found in Jane Austen or Dickens, for a more 'stream of consciousness' approach which focussed not on outward events but on the reaction of the mind of the main characters to those events. So this is not a given traditional narrative in which Shekhar – like the boatman I described in the previous chapter – can find his identity ready made. Instead he has to construct the narrative himself and in the making of it discover who he is. We must beware of over-simplifying and so of making this contrast appear to be absolute. In many novels and certainly in this one, it is possible to discern a spectrum of smaller internal narratives which define identity with increasing degrees of intensity. It will be useful at this point to describe this spectrum. It is inevitably a somewhat arbitrary construct and the boundaries between the different categories within it are not as sharply defined as my analysis suggests.

At one end of it are people like the villagers of Gangauli and the Ganges boatman. Their identities are defined, but also confined, with a traditional structure of both story and social status or caste, and very often of local community too. Such characters can be found in the pages of a novel but they belong essentially to the world to whose passing the very existence of the novel testifies.[6] We can call these first narratives 'narratives of type', for the individuals they describe are hardly different from many other people like themselves. Next there are what I will

---

[6]In the previous chapter I quoted Fuentes' claim that the novel could not exist in societies characterised by the unitary vision of epic.

call 'narratives of external identity' which in a rather
external and factual way do describe who a separate individual is. At the beginning of the first chapter I identified
myself in this way by telling part of the story of my time
in India.

Our next move along the spectrum is to narratives
which begin to describe identity more fully and more in-
wardly. I call these 'narratives of renewal', and I want to
examine them at some length. In Ajneya's novels it sometimes happens that a character describes a painful experience in the presence of a sympathetic listener. The listening makes the painful experience into one of healing and
renewal for it can now be included in the story of who the
sufferer is, instead of being simply meaningless and ab-
surd. Thus it modifies and enriches the original story. The
teller of the story has moved some way along the road to
becoming what in modern western terms I would describe
as a whole and integrated person. I am not suggesting that
as a universal model to which everyone in all societies
ought to aspire. That would simply be a new kind of impe-
rialism, but it is still significant and needs to be compared
with, and criticised in the light of other models of what it
means to be a human being.

There is a good example of such a narrative of renewal in the story of Shashi, who is one of the main characters of Ajneya's novel. Indeed, she is almost its heroine
in a way that Shekhar is not its hero. We have seen that
Shashi is a childhood friend of Shekhar. She is also a
relation and may be his cousin, but their precise blood
relationship is, perhaps deliberately, left unclear. As I have
already pointed out, they meet for a second time after an
interval of many years when Shekhar comes to study in
Lahore, which is where Shashi and her parents live. Her

father dies and during Shekhar's first spell in jail her
widowed mother arranges an unsatisfactory marriage for
her. Her husband is shallow and superficial in character
and westernised in his habits. He spends most of his time
drinking at the local club with his friends. He is uncouth
and brutal in his treatment of Shashi and wholly mistrust-
ful of her. He literally kicks her out of his flat when he
thinks, quite wrongly, that she has been misbehaving herself with Shekhar, who by now is out of prison. Shekhar
takes her into his own one room and but for this welcome
and acceptance of her suicide would have been a real possibility. According to Hindu tradition, a woman should
never leave her husband however badly he may treat her[7],
and a woman whom her husband had disowned had no-
where else to go. In the period when this novel was written
it would have been unthinkable for her to return to her own
family.

Eventually, she manages to tell Shekhar the story of
her wretched marriage, emphasising that the act of marry-
ing this man at all was a sacrifice which she had made
willingly and with her eyes open.[8] Although she does not
actually say so she seems to realise that Shekhar needs to
know and accept this part of her experience if he is to
share her life now. The novel implicity claims that her
telling of the story, and his acceptance of it without con-
demning her, open up the possibility of, and provide the
moral justification for their new life together. That justification cannot be set within the framework of the old

---

[7]*Manusmriti* 5.154. For an English translation of this work
see W Doniger and B K Smith, *The Laws of Manu*, Penguin
Books, London and New York, 1991.

[8]The theme of sacrifice is developed in the next chapter.

social structures. What Ajneya seems to be proposing here is a new morality based not on traditional assumptions but on common human values: a woman as unjustly treated as Shashi had been, and one who had been literally thrown out of the house by her husband as well, surely had the right to appeal to a protector, especially a protector who was a relation, and who would live with her in a purely platonic relationship – Shekhar and Shashi do not have sexual relations.

It is the story of her suffering which is the foundation of the new identity which Shashi discovers in being Shekhar's partner. Indeed she becomes much more than a partner. She believes in Shekhar's vocation to write even when he cannot believe in it himself. She saves him from suicide at a moment of despair. She eventually dies from the injuries which she sustained when her husband threw her out – it's that sort of book ! At the beginning of the novel, when Shekhar is looking back over his past life, he claims that it was she who made him, and at the end he describes her as his eternal inspiration and the giver of *moksha* – that ultimate release which is in the Hindu tradition the goal of all spiritual endeavour. Of course Shekhar does not mean that because, as we shall see in a moment, in his view there is and can be nothing after this life, so he is using a traditional term in a secular way. He is also using it in a radical way, because in the tradition woman is very often one of the great obstacles on men's path to *moksha*. This is one example of the way in which this writer re-interprets his inheritance in the act of rebelling against it.

At this point I refer to what I touched on in passing in the previous chapter: a novel is written in a particular context with a particular readership in mind, but in a new context new readers may perceive in it themes of which the author may not have been aware. Thus in the West and increasingly in India too the whole question of the relationship between women and men is now openly discussed in a way that was not possible when this novel was first written. Thus Ajneya's concerns in the India of the nineteen forties are not very far removed from some of ours today.[9] To put our own concerns in a larger and cross-cultural perspective is to see them through new eyes. So here is another example of the new possibilities for dialogue and mutual understanding which a novel can open up.

But we must return to our narrative spectrum: can we begin to see the various points on it as stages on a journey, a journey we can perhaps describe as being from 'type' to 'personhood' ? The 'type' fits into the traditional world of 'epic vision' within which she or he plays out a largely traditional role. The 'person' cannot belong to that world in the same way, and has indeed moved outside it. The way back into it is barred by self-awareness. Ajneya himself indirectly endorses this interpretation. In 1959 he contributed an article on Hindi literature to a volume of essays on the then current state of writing in the various regional languages of India. The article is in English and at one point he writes about the period after 1918. He says:

---

[9]In western societies co-habitation without marriage is becoming increasingly common. At the heart of marriage in both Christianity and Hinduism is an exclusive and life-long commitment of a woman and a man to one another which is publicly made before God. I believe as a priest that my pastoral responsibility is not to reject and condemn those who settle for something less than that commitment by choosing co-habitation, but to encourage them to marry.

[T]he search for personality [which] was, consciously
or unconsciously the main driving force of the literature of the period and the source of its bitterness and
absurdities, its exasperations and exaltations.

In a tradition where the age had always been more
important than the artist, literature had inevitably been
concerned more with the creation of types than of
individuals...As the Hindi writer discovered himself
as an individual he became aware that as a creator he
was concerned with persons. The realisation was as
painful as the discovery had been awkward and em-
barrassing: the degree of maturity and poise in subsequent writing directly reflects the degree and speed
of the adjustment which the individual writer was able
to attain with the new situation.[10]

Now I want to suggest that this shift is of considerable
interest and importance for Christians, for while in one
sense a concern with persons as self-conscious individuals
is modern and goes back only to the Romantic Movement
at the beginning of the last century, in another and more
important sense a concern with persons in relationship lies
at the heart of the Christian vision of life. For example,
within the New Testament much of the writing of St. Paul
is concerned with the establishing of relationships between
people in the communities which he founded, relationships
which in his view must be governed by the nature of faith
in Christ. If that be true then it follows that a literary
concern with the significance of persons in another tradition opens up rich possibilities of conversation. That pos-

---

[10]S H Vatsyayan, 'Hindi Literature', in *Contemporary Indian Literature: a Symposium*, Sahitya Akademi, New Delhi,
1957, second edition, revised and enlarged, 1959, p 84.

sibility is intimately linked with the parallel shift from epic to the novel as a literary form which I described in the previous chapter. At the same time I am aware that this view of personhood is challenged in two ways from within the Indian tradition. First, the traditional pattern of the joint family fits much more easily within the first place on my narrative spectrum, with the individual as a representative 'type', and secondly *Advaita Vedanta* offers a profoundly different understanding of what it means to be a human being. This is to underline what I wrote above, about the dangers of assuming that the western model of personhood is or should be universal.

With that important caveat in mind we note that awareness of oneself as a person reaches a climax at the last point of our spectrum which is exemplified by this novel itself as a whole. The act of writing the story of his whole life is Shekhar's only way of discovering who he is. Hence the urgency of writing of it in the face of death, with its threat of finally destroying all identity. On the first page of the novel Shekhar says:

> I am looking back on my life, reliving my past life. I, who always kept on looking forwards, having arrived at the final stage of my life's journey, am looking back to where I started from, and how, forgetful and straying, and through many strange experiences, I arrived at where I am now. (Vol 1 p 15).

The Introduction to the novel appears over the author's own signature, which thus separates it from the narrative proper. At the end of this Introduction Ajneya writes:

> Shekhar is not a great man, he is not even a good man, but in the light of humanity's accumulated experience he honestly tries to recognise himself. And, who

knows, in this modern age when you and I and everyone else is a composite character, you may even find
that within you is a Shekhar, who is neither great nor
good, but who is alert and free and honest, above all
honest. (Vol 1 p 12)

So here is an explicit invitation to the readers to see themselves as it were reflected in this story of a particular
individual and so to use Shekhar's narrative to understand
and make sense of their own lives. This means that our
spectrum begins to look not like a straight line but a circle,
for here is a use of the novel which is similar to the
function of that epic vision which I described in the first
Lecture. It becomes a story within which an individual
reader can find meaning, only now it is meaning of a very
personal kind, and far from being already given is one
which the individual must construct for him or herself.

Let us now look a little more closely at Shekhar's life.
Because he can be critical both of himself and of his tradition, he is the kind of person with whom I can engage in
a conversation or dialogue. This is true of him in a way
that was not true of any of the characters of Gangauli
whom I described in the previous chapter. Shekhar is involved in questioning, rejecting, and to a degree in reshaping his own tradition and that is an enterprise for which I
have great sympathy, for is it not what all people of religion are called upon in different ways to do today? Here
again, we must be wary of making absolute distinctions:
every living tradition is continually going through that
process of reshaping and redefinition. Indeed, only if I am
involved in that process within my own tradition, and you
are in yours, can we really meet. Otherwise all we can do
is try to impose our own unitary and exclusive views on
one another. What then are the particular elements in

Shekhar's criticism of his own inheritance from which we can learn ? In the remainder of this chapter I want to examine three of them.

First, he reshapes the parameters within which human life is understood as being lived. Early in the novel he says to himself:

> Science says that life comes only once, and that no part of human life is eternal, in death the whole of it comes to an end, nothing remains which could be reborn. All around him is suffering, poverty, pain, disease, death, everything. The touts of religion in different countries have exhausted all their creative powers in devising the most fearful and evil torments in hell, but they are all in the world, there in his world, and he does not accept them, he rebels and fights against them. (Vol 1 p 72)

So here is a criticism not just of his own Hindu tradition, but of mine and of all others. I have to accept that in part he is right. The traditional pictures of heaven and hell, whether Hindu or Christian were, to a large extent, devised by the powerful as a means of social control. Yet at the same time I have to part company with Shekhar for I believe we have to insist on human accountability to someone or something beyond ourselves, whom I would call God, though we cannot now do that by using the traditional pictures of heaven and hell. In other words, for me as a Christian, the concept of some kind of final judgment, however understood, is an essential element in the faith which I profess. In the end I am answerable for the life I have lived. Shekhar compels me to rethink what such accountability might mean.

Further, I believe Shekhar is right to insist that we

take this world seriously as having ultimate value and
meaning for its own sake: 'Suffering, poverty, disease,
pain and death', which he lists, are indeed some of the
great enemies with which we have to do battle. We can no
longer justify these things as the necessary preparation for
an after-life, nor can we draw their sting by claiming that
a better life after death will compensate for them, nor can
we explain them away as being caused by previous bad
karma, or as being simply *maya*, to use two traditional and
important Hindu terms. On the other hand I cannot agree
with Shekhar in his insistence that this life is all that there
is. Yet we can only with honesty believe in a life to come
if that belief does not ignore, or simply afford a compen-
sation for the horrors which many people have to endure in
this one.

A second element in Shekhar's criticism, and one
closely related to the first, is that he rejects the social
boundaries which separated people from one another,
boundaries which in traditional Hindu society used to be
marked by the concept of ritual purity.[11] Purity regulations
played a dominant role in the lives of the Sanskrit pundits
of Varanasi at whose feet I sat as a student for those six
years in the seventies. Shekhar's rejection of this concept
is made clear in several incidents.

One of them occurs while he is a teen-age student in
Madras.[12] As a Brahmin he eats in the Brahmin students'
dining hall but he refuses to conform to traditional regulations. He notices how this hall is protected from even the

---

[11]This concept is found in most religions, if not in all. A
comparative study could prove very illuminating.

[12]This was before the Dravida Kazhagam and other move-
ments had effectively challenged Brahmin supremacy.

glance of a lowcaste person, but the Brahmin students are quite happy to drive away with a 'shoo' the occasional dog which creeps into the hall. In other words in their eyes people of lower caste are less even than dogs. Eventually, Shekhar's refusal to conform becomes too much for the other students:

> He began to notice that all the students were looking at him as if he were some kind of strange creature and it seemed to him that in their hearts they were wondering what he would be in his next birth – a dog or a crow or a worm – and as if they were filled with compassion for his fate. The thought of this compassion made him fume and he thought to himself: 'If I am going to hell where are they going ?'

> But their compassion did not soften their hearts to the extent that the thought of his going to hell made them forget their own prospects for the other world. They decided that they would no longer eat with Shekhar and one day he discovered that they had all submitted a petition to the Principal asking him to make separate arrangements for him. They said that if this request was not granted they would be compelled to leave the hostel. (Vol 1 pp 207-8)

That incident reminds me of the verse of a hymn which English Christians of my generation used to sing in church when we were children:

> The rich man in his castle, the poor man at his gate, God made them high and lowly and ordered their estate.[13]

---

[13]The hymn – 'All things bright and beautiful' – is still sung; but nowadays this verse is omitted.

I wrote above that I can only engage in dialogue with a
Shekhar because he is engaged in a critical dialogue with
his own inheritance. For the dialogue to be genuine I have
to do the same and be critical of my own. I am not advo-
cating here a competition in horror stories: you tell me
something bad about your religion and I respond by telling
you something even worse about mine. Conversations of
that kind are always rather unreal, though sometimes they
are necessary at the early stages of meeting. I am proposing something rather more subtle and I hope more profound
than that. When I see something bad in your tradition I
must look for something bad in my own, not in order to
compete, but to make the point that I too stand under that
judgment of whose necessity I have already written. In
Christian language I want to say that we both stand under
the judgment of God and that I must not attempt to play
God by setting myself up as your judge. That is my basis
for establishing a relationship of equality.

In our novel Shekhar rejects the use of religion and
indeed the creation of religious texts to suppress the poor,
and to justify both their continuing poverty and the con-
tempt with which they are treated. At one point he is writing a book of social criticism, and he calls it *Hamara
Samaj, Our Society*. He buys a copy of the Laws of Manu
precisely in order to criticise it, for it is in this text that he
finds the root of the social oppression against which he is
protesting. We have already noted that Manu explicitly
says that a woman must stay with her husband however
badly he may behave. In Shekhar's criticism of Manu and
my criticism of my own Christian tradition, there is common ground. To identify it we must return briefly to Hans
Frei whom I quoted in the first chapter. Frei pointed out
that in the eighteenth century in Europe some people began
to see that the Bible as traditionally understood could no

longer encompass the whole of reality. They became aware
of, 'another temporal reality than the biblical'. Within this
space it became both necessary and possible to write a new
kind of narrative, the novel. It also became possible to
look at the Bible in a new way and to use its material for
historical investigation. So there could begin the use of the
Gospels for the 'quest of the historical Jesus'. These meth-
ods are also being applied to the Hindu scriptures. On my
shelves I have one such book entitled *The Rise of the
Religious Significance of Rama*,[14] which traces the development of the figure of Rama through the various versions
of the Epic. That is a process which the boatman whom I
described in the first chapter could not have understood.
But Shekhar could have understood it, for his own study of
the Laws of Manu makes similar assumptions.

To Shekhar we now return in order to consider the
third area of his criticism which concerns his attitude to
women. We have already touched on this in our examina-
tion of the way in which he welcomes the rejected Shashi
into his room, and in the pattern of their subsequent life
together. At an earlier stage of the novel he makes his
criticism of traditional attitudes to women more explicit.
After he has been expelled from the Brahmin hostel in
Madras he gathers around him a circle of like-minded fel-
low-students from the scheduled caste hostel. They meet
together to discuss the problems of the day – as indeed
students the world over have always done. On one occa-
sion Shekhar says to the little company:

It will be necessary to destroy the self-satisfaction of
this male-dominated society and to show that its self-

---

[14]F Whaling, *The Rise of the Religious Significance of Rama*,
Motilal Banarsidass, Delhi, Varansasi, Patna, 1980.

righteousness is false, only then will we find the path by **which we can go** forward (Vol 1 p 218)

In 1997 such sentiments seem so obvious that they are almost a cliche, but they were anything but a cliche in 1941, when the first volume of this novel was published. This is an example of the way in which novelists can sometimes be prophetic figures, seeing deeper into the issues of their own time than their contemporaries are able to do, and so able to see further ahead as well.

To sum up: we have already seen reason to question the adequacy of both the exclusive and the inclusive types of epic vision. In this chapter we have seen the rich possibilities which a critical individual vision can offer as Shekhar struggles to find himself as a human being and to redefine the society in which he lives. In the final chapter I want to use what we have learnt from the village of Gangauli and from the story of Shekhar and to ask if there are other ways in which we can more effectively tell the stories of the human communities to which we belong, and so 'narrate our nations', especially in the context of suffering. Here too, I shall argue that Christian insights can illuminate and deepen the discussion.

CHAPTER THREE :
Listening to the Victims

I begin this final chapter by standing back from the novels
we have discussed so far and setting them in a larger
context. I have been looking at the question: how do we
tell the stories of who we are, and how through those
stories can we define the identities of our nations ? I have
also been suggesting that there are important ways in which
Christian insights can illuminate this question. In the first
chapter we looked at it in the light of Rahi Masoom Reza's
Half the Village. Reza, a Shi'i Muslim, told the story of a
typical part of his community in order to argue that they
have as much right to be in India as any one else, and that
the majority must not be allowed to define themselves in a
way which either excludes minorities or turns them into
second class citizens. That is what minorities, or weak
communities often do. They demand of the powerful — who
are usually, though not always, the majority — a new form
of inclusive self-definition, and that is something the powerful are usually reluctant to concede, for it seems to them
to put their own identity at risk. This has a relevance far
beyond India. To quote two obvious contemporary examples: whites in South Africa until recently, and Jews in
Israel still, have tried to define themselves, to narrate their
version of what the nation is, in a way which either excludes Black people in the one case and Palestinians in the
other, or else reduces them to second class status.

This issue also presses upon us in Britain. It is now becoming increasingly difficult if not impossible for the English, of whom I am one, to define ourselves in a way which ignores the Scots, the Welsh and the Irish. Further, there are now substantial numbers of British Muslims, Hindus and Sikhs, to say nothing of the Jews. In 1988 there was a debate in the British House of Lords[1] about a new Education Bill in which the government tried to impose an act of compulsory Christian worship on all state-controlled schools. A contribution to that debate was made by a Jewish peer, Lord Beloff. He said that he was worried by some of the speeches made in support of the motion. He pointed out that he himself belonged to a minority community and there had been references to the Christian nation and a Christian country

> such that a person like myself, and people who believed themselves to be part of this nation, although practising different religious faiths, are somehow second class citizens.[2]

We have looked at some possible and some impossible answers to the question of how we live together. One answer which worked in a satisfactory way in many places for a very long time was exemplified by the Shi'i community of Gangauli. They told and indeed actually lived the story of Moharrum in a way which could include both Hindus of high or low caste, as well as Sunni Muslims. I have argued that the Gangauli solution is no longer viable and that Reza's novel can be read as an elegy for its passing. Modern education, the influence of the mass me-

---

[1] The House of Lords has a similar role to that of India's Rajya Sabha.

[2] The Independent, Tuesday, 17th May, 1988. The Independent is a major British daily newspaper.

dia, and the modern economy which compels people to leave their Gangaulis to find work, all make it very difficult if not actually impossible to sustain in the long run the isolation on which the Gangaulis of this world have depended in order to maintain their inclusive unitary vision of the village community.

So where do we go from Gangauli? Whatever our final destination we can only get to it by way, so to speak, of *Shekhar: a Life.* Shekhar found himself no longer at home in his Hindu equivalent of Gangauli and its collective story. He was not simply exiled from but radically critical of much in his Brahminical Hindu inheritance. He reshapes the transcendental and social boundaries within which life is understood as being lived. He rejects traditional belief in heaven and hell and sees these as simply the way in which the powerful kept those beneath them in a state of subservience. He rejects discrimination based on caste, and the rituals of purity which embody and define caste divisions. He rejects the unquestioning subservience of women to men and in particular of a wife to her husband as laid down in the Laws of Manu. Instead he takes Shashi into his room when she has been thrown out of her own home by her brutal and jealous husband. In doing so he has broken a taboo and crossed a social Rubicon, and so has she. They have put themselves outside the boundaries of what is socially acceptable. When they have done so their roles are reversed: he had saved her by giving her a home, but now she saves him from suicide and becomes the inspiration for the writing to which he increasingly feels himself committed. Here we see Shashi and Shekhar together struggling for a reshaping of the relation between women and men. That struggle, in one way or another, is now happening, at no little personal cost to all who are involved in it, in many traditional societies across the world. Ajneya published the two volumes of Shekhar in 1941 and 1944. So here is an example of the point which I made in the first chapter: a novel can sometimes speak more profoundly and with more relevance in a new context than it could do in the one to which it was originally addressed.

As contemporary people it is no longer open to us to belong in our inherited religious traditions in the unselfconscious and uncritical way in which the residents of Gangauli did and in many places still do. I want to claim that there is no turning back on that self-consciousness which Shekhar represents and embodies, but I am very much aware that I write as a westerner who therefore puts a high value on the notion of the responsible independent person. In the last chapter I was able to claim the support of Ajneya in that emphasis, but that does not mean that we are both irrefutably right. But assuming for the purposes of my argument that we are, we must again refine our question: how do we narrate our nations 'post-Shekhar' whether in a limited political sense or in a more profound religious sense?

First let us look briefly at the political context: it is perhaps surprising that our three novels all simply take it for granted that it is the nation which we have to narrate, for the modern nation-state is a nineteenth century European invention. Arguably it is a far more significant legacy to India and other countries which were the objects of colonialism than colonialism itself ever was. It is an irony that those who opposed colonialism did so in the name of the nation-state, for in doing so they chose to do battle on their opponents' ground. In a valuable study, *Nations and Nationalism since 1780*,[3] the historian Eric Hobsbawm

---

[3] E J Hobsbawm, *Nations and Nationalism since 1780*, Cambridge University Press, Cambridge, 1990.

points out some characteristics of the nation-state: he says that it 'differs in size, scale and nature from the actual communities with which human beings have identified over most of history, and makes quite different demands of them'. (p 46) Because modern governments directly administer vast numbers of citizens, and because of modern technical and economic developments, the inhabitants of the nation-state need to be turned into citizens and that implies a degree of homogenisation and standardisation. So universal literacy is desirable and the mass development of secondary education almost mandatory. Nation-states need a national language which everybody speaks. Hobsbawm points out that national languages could not exist at all before the era of universal primary education. They are, he suggests, almost always semi-artificial constructs and indeed sometimes, like modern Hebrew, they are virtually invented. In an important passage he says:

> They are the opposite of what nationalist mythology supposes them to be, namely the primordial foundations of national culture and the matrices of the national mind. They are usually attempts to devise a standardised idiom out of a multiplicity of actually spoken idioms. (p 54)

The same is true of course of the modern Hindi language.

Finally and not least, Hobsbawm observes that turning subjects into citizens means democratising politics. Everyone has the vote and this

> tends to produce a populist consciousness which, seen in some lights, is hard to distinguish from a national, even a chauvinist patriotism – for if the country is in some way 'mine' then it is more readily seen as preferable to those of foreigners. (p 88)

In all the novels we have been considering the nation-state in the broad sense is taken for granted as that to which India aspires. It is never questioned or even explained as an ideal, or as the appropriate way for contemporary human beings to live together and share a common life. The use of vocabulary provides confirmation of this argument. Consider the word *desh*: in Hindu philosophy it usually means 'place', as in the phrase 'place and time'. In the Puranas and Epics it often means the place or land where a group of people live, and sometimes it is used to refer to India – *Bharat* – as a whole. In our novels, however, the word is almost personified. Its meaning has been extended to mean not just the land itself but those who live on it, their history and their culture. Thus the *desh* is in slavery to foreigners and so its freedom is a desirable goal for which people are willing to make sacrifices. It inspires devotion (*bhakti*), and can be prayed for. This extension of meaning simply happens, the case for it is not argued.

Rarely if ever does a particular nation completely embody the ideal of being a society of equal citizens. As the three examples of South Africa, Israel and Britain, demonstrate, there are always within it groups which do not fit the mould. Further, with the rejection of a hierarchy where every person and every group had its place and its role laid down by tradition, as was often the case in the past, different groups now compete for limited resources. We saw evidence of that at the end of Reza's novel, when the *zamindari* system was abolished. This meant that the Shi'i Muslims who stayed in the village after 1947 lost their social status and had to curry favour from a Chamar villager who was now an MLA. We also saw in the last chapter how Shekhar challenged traditional hierarchical ideals of society. He appeals to something like natural justice rather than to any ideal of the nation state. Yet he is very much involved in India's struggle for freedom and indeed is under sentence of death for having pursued that goal by violent means.

The nation state's rejection of hierarchy and its insistence that all are now equal citizens with one vote each has an important consequence. In a situation of burgeoning population figures and inevitably limited resources, competition between groups becomes more and more intense. Here we have a paradox: the very openness and freedom of opportunity to which the nation-state aspires opens up, at least in theory, new avenues and opportunities to the members of minority communities. Yet this very freedom makes the minorities more of a threat to others and so often more vulnerable to hostility and persecution than they were before. For example, the British historian David Thomson points out that in the Russia of the 1870s Jews were allowed to come out of their ghettos and to move about more freely, but it was this very freedom which led in the next decade to anti-Semitic measures and even pogroms.[4] In other words Jews confined to their ghettos, where they had lived for centuries, were poor and suffered discrimination, but in the eyes of the rest of society they were 'safe' because under control. When they were allowed to leave the ghettos and compete with everyone else on level terms they were perceived to be a threat.

In societies which aspire to provide equal opportunities for all, and where in the nature of things there are not enough goods and opportunities to go round, we have a situation of competition in which every group sees itself

---

[4]D Thomson, *Europe Since Napoleon*, (First published by Longman's 1957), Revised Edition, Penguin Books, London, 1990, p 482.

as being threatened by other groups. Groups which feel
themselves to be the losers very quickly start to define
themselves as victims. In an important and thought-pro-
voking book about communal trouble in Hyderabad the
psycho-analyst Sudhir Kakar reflects on this situation in
the light of Freud's concept of the 'chosen trauma'. He
writes:

> [The] chosen trauma does not mean that either the
> Hindus or the Muslims chose to become victims but
> only that they have 'chosen' to mythologise, psycho-
> logically internalise and thus constantly dwell upon a
> particular event from their history. A chosen trauma
> is reactivated again and again to strengthen a group's
> cohesiveness through 'memories' of its persecution,
> victimisation, and eventual survival.[5]

Now here we come to the heart of the problem of narrating
the nation today: the dominant community cannot tell its
story in a way which includes minorities if at the same
time it perceives itself as the victim of, or at least as
threatened by, other groups. To tell an inclusive story we
need to feel and believe that we are secure. Being victims,
or perceiving ourselves as victims, is precisely about being, or at least feeling, insecure. It can also be about the
refusal of responsibility for if we see ourselves as perpet-
ual victims then everything is always someone else's fault,
never our own, and so there is no need for us to be held
accountable and responsible for what we do. Now it would
be irresponsible of me to suggest that I had some simple
solution to resolve this dilemma. I offer nothing as foolish
or ambitious as that. What I want to offer in the rest of this

---

[5]S Kakar, *The Colours of Violence*, Viking, New Delhi,
1995, p 63.

final chapter – with the help of the novels – are some clues
towards that 'strategy of resistance' to which I have already referred.

My first clue is this: all the great religions offer their
adherents a path of growth into spiritual maturity and personal wholeness. I am not at this point going to argue
about the theological status of that self-awareness in the
context of the conflicting truth claims of the different faiths.
Important though that issue is, especially for Christians,
for the purpose of my argument I am leaving it on one side.
Instead I am simply pointing to the self-evident fact that
the faiths do offer their followers a way to maturity, and
that such maturity necessarily includes a degree of self-
awareness. In the Hindu tradition, for example, you normally need a *guru*, who will help you along the path of life,
but the true *guru* and the one who is right for you is always
hard to find. He will not advertise himself, it is up to you
to go and look for him. My Hindu friends are scathing
about those whom they describe as 'jet-set' *gurus* who
have become big names in the West and attracted many
followers – and a lot of money. Now that deliberate
hiddenness of the ideal *guru* suggests that he does not
depend for his identity in having people who consult him.
If he did he would have to go out and look for them.
Further, the Hindu myths are full of stories of great holy
men who are so to speak knocked off their perches and
reduced to normal status. Indeed the gods, and in particular
Indra, are not above sending glamorous heavenly damsels
to distract them from their devotions. It is possible to
interpret these stories in a variety of different ways. One
way is to read them as making the point that holiness is
never a permanent achievement, and that the line between
holiness and its opposite is much thinner than those who
aspire to holiness often realise.

I want to argue that the kind of self-awareness which
the great traditions all in their different ways make available to those who live within them needs to be purified and
enlarged by that peculiarly modern kind of self-discovery
which we looked at in *Shekhar: a Life*. To make this point
in more general terms: it is good to be loyal to our traditions, but in the modern world if our loyalty is to be genuine it must also be critical. An excellent example of this
attitude is to be found in Sudhir Kakar himself. He calls
himself as a 'liberal rationalist (with a streak of Gnostic
mysticism)'.[6] He describes the appalling horrors which he
witnessed as a boy of nine in the Partition massacres of
1947[7], and yet he writes with a depth of compassion and a
breadth of understanding which I wish a few more of my
fellow-Christian believers would emulate. One of the marks
of the self-aware in the sense that I have been describing
is that they have the detachment and inner security which
can potentially enable them to listen to the victims tell
their stories, without being threatened and fearful themselves.

Here I return briefly to the previous chapter in which
I set out a spectrum of narratives of identity. I referred
to 'narratives of renewal', several of which were to be
found in *Shekhar a Life*. In these narratives a character
described a painful experience in the hearing of a sympathetic listener and in the process found a measure of
healing and recreation. (Jungian and other forms of
psychotherapy are based on that principle.) I could equally
well have called these 'narratives of the victim'. Almost
by definition a victim is left out and forgotten. In *Shekhar:
a Life* there are several characters who would have been

---

[6]*op. cit.* p 214.
[7]*ibid.* pp 31-43.

forgotten if their story had not been told. At one point in
the novel Shekhar is having one of his periodic bouts of
despair and says he has nothing to write about. Shashi, as
always, is by his side to encourage and inspire. She says
to him:

> I cannot agree that there is no material for you to
> write about. You haven't forgotten it, you are refus-
> ing to look at it. Is there nothing to write about Baba
> Madansingh ? Did you get nothing from Mohasin which
> in future could be given to others ? Is Rama-ji not
> worth writing about ? (Vol 2 p 217)

All three of the characters to whom Shashi refers were
people whom Shekhar had met in jail, and all in different
ways had made a deep impression on him. They were all
outsiders, who no longer fitted into contemporary society.
Madansingh was a wise old man and a long-term political
prisoner. Mohasin, a Muslim, was another political
prisoner and he inspired everyone else by his courage under
punishment and his irrepressible cheerfulness. Rama-ji was
somewhat different. He was on death's row when Shekhar
befriended him. He had upheld the family honour by killing
a man who had an affair with his brother's wife while his
brother was away from the village. Shekhar envied him,
his certainty and confidence that he had done the right
thing. Unlike Shekhar himself he did not have to carry the
burden of self-awareness with its corollary of doubt, question, inner conflict and anguish. In other words Rama-ji is
still living mentally in the Hindu equivalent of Gangauli
while Shekhar himself has stepped out of it and knows that
there is no way back.

A Christian will want to see a theological significance in the fact that Shashi urges Shekhar to write these
stories: if the story of the victim is told then the meaning

of events no longer rests with the oppressor. Though the events when they happened were not in the control of the victim their meaning now is. That suggests that these 'narratives of the victim' belong to a *genre* which is not far from the passion story of Christ. For the four Evangelists tell their story in such a way that the meaning of events is now vested in the victim. Pilate, the soldiers, the crowd, the religious leaders, are made part of the story of Christ. It is now not their story but his and they are only in it because he is.

Here we can learn much from another novel, *A False Truth*, by the Marxist writer Yashpal. It is written on a vast canvas and its two volumes together amount to over a thousand pages. Yashpal sets his first volume in the context of Bholapande Gali, a lower middle-class area of Lahore. In some ways this is an urban and Hindu equivalent of Shi'i Gangauli. Yashpal describes how the lives of people who live in this *gali* are overtaken and uprooted by the terrible events of Partition in 1947. After appalling suffering most of them make their way to the newly-independent India where some of them in the end — and this is especially true of the women — actually enjoy a life of greater freedom, prosperity and achievement than they ever knew, or could have known, if the pattern of their lives had continued undisturbed in Lahore.

Yashpal is at pains throughout this novel to tell the story of the victims and in so doing to challenge the dominant account of the events of these years by providing what in his view is a more honest and convincing alternative. While he is not directly addressing the situation of contemporary democratic societies where many groups perceive themselves as victims, which I described above, his novel can be profitably read with that context in mind. He has little good to say of Gandhi, Nehru or the Congress Party, who are the heroes of the dominant account of the period with which he deals. Whom then does he see as the victims? They are first of all the poor. The first person who had connections with Bholapande Gali to die in the communal violence which gripped Lahore in 1947 was old Daula Mamu the Muslim fruit-seller. The Hindu children of the gali all loved him and when the festival of Holi began he was always the first to have coloured water thrown over him. His death was quickly followed by that of a Hindu shoe-mender who earned his living sitting at the road-side. On a wider scale it was Punjabis who bore the brunt of events. They flock to Delhi in their thousands as refugees, but their sufferings are not acknowledged by those who have always lived in Delhi. Indeed, one of them remarks: 'We people are becoming a sacrifice (balidan). These people [ie the indigenous inhabitants of Delhi] are gaining the benefit of offering up other people in sacrifice'. (Vol 1 p 404) There is a striking reshaping of traditional language and imagery here. The speaker uses the Sanskrit word which is commonly used to describe the Vedic sacrifice which was the basis of ancient Hinduism. Here it is personalised and used in a new and historical context.

We must not see that contrast between ancient and modern as too stark or absolute. In a fascinating and important study called *Victory to the Mother*,[8] K M Erndl describes the evolution of devotion to the mother goddess in her various forms in North-Western India. She describes how the leader of a group of devotees in Chandigarh told

---

[8]K M Erndl, *Victory to the Mother: The Hindu Goddess of Northwest India in Myth, Ritual and Symbol*, Oxford University Press, New York, Oxford, 1993.

of a king who had to sacrifice his own son in order to
discover the secret of how a particular lamp was lit. The
leader went on to interpret this sacrifice in the following
terms:

> The idea is that everything belongs to and comes from
> Devi (the goddess). Balidan means getting rid of your
> ego. One has to extinguish the self. One shouldn't
> say, 'This is mine'.(p 97)

So here too there is a similar reshaping of the traditional
vocabulary of sacrifice to the one we are discussing, but it
happens in a context where those concerned are closely in
touch with their tradition in a way in which Yashpal and
his main characters are not. To return to Yashpal: among
the victims are the Communists, or ex-Communists with
prison records, whose contribution to the freedom struggle
is forgotten and who very often cannot get jobs in the new
India. One such is a young man called Gill. He was of Sikh
parentage and for the sake of the girl he loved, who was
not a Sikh, cut his hair and shaved his beard. He was
expelled from his orthodox home, but also from the Com-
munist Party on the grounds that what he had done would
alienate ordinary Sikhs from the Party. His fiancee was
killed during the Partition massacres. He meets with Kanak,
a Hindu girl, when both are about to be interviewed for a
job in Delhi. Gill realises that Kanak is in a far more
desperate situation than he is and so withdraws his appli-
cation so that she can get the job.

Yashpal implies in this story that in the midst of all
this horror and mayhem there are people of integrity who
are prepared to make sacrifices for the sake of others, but
that suffering is the inevitable price they pay for being the
kind of people they are in these sort of circumstances.
They are victims – though in the case of Gill and those like

him, they are victims not by mere force of circumstances
but by their own deliberate choice. They make their stand
open-eyed, knowing what the cost will be. They refuse to
be simply caught up in events. The story Yashpal tells is
their story. He narrates the nation from their point of view
and thus subverts the dominant version of events.

In Yashpal's story the greatest sufferers are women,
and the woman who suffers most is the Hindu Tara. In the
first volume she is a college student and belongs with most
of her friends to the left-wing Student's Federation in
Lahore. There she falls in love with a young Muslim called
Asad. One day they both attend the naming ceremony of a
Sikh baby, the young relative of one of their college friends.
Both of them find this ceremony totally meaningless and
they catch one another's eye across the boundary line which
separates the men from the women in the room where it
takes place. The ceremony itself is ridiculed. Asad, like
everyone else, is given a lump of sticky sweet *prasada* to
eat and has nothing to wipe his hands on. Tara slips him a
handkerchief. Behind this description is the implicit claim
that if people can shed the ridiculous mumbo-jumbo imposed by traditional forms of religion then they can find
their real unity in a shared humanity. But when it comes to
the moment of decision Asad does not have courage to
break with tradition and marry Tara. Her family, who are
also prisoners of tradition, arrange a marriage for her
against her will with a corrupt, violent, poorly educated
and communally minded young man called Somraj. There
is nothing to choose between him and Shashi's husband in.
Shekhar: a Life.[9]

---

[9]In many Hindi novels of this period the violent and boorish
husband in an arranged marriage is very much a stock and
stylised character.

Because of the tense political situation Tara's marriage is a necessarily low-key affair and is over-taken by violence. Her husband is beating her up on their wedding night when a Muslim mob bursts into the house. She is rescued from the mob and a Muslim family take her into their home. Here she is well treated but the Muslims try to convert her and when they see that they will not succeed they tell her they are going to send her to a refugee camp for Hindus. Tara goes through the most appalling suffering, including rape, and eventually ends up in Delhi where she struggles, successfully in the end, to build a new life for herself as an independent career women.

What is significant for our purposes is that her experience is often described in the traditional language of sacrifice. When faced with Asad's spinelessness and the pressure of her family on her to marry Somraj she complains: 'All these people think it is their *dharma* and duty to offer me in sacrifice'.(Vol 1 p 215) Here the word for sacrifice is *kurban*. A few pages later Yashpal describes how one day she returns home as 'reluctantly as an animal being led to the place of slaughter'. (Vol 1 p 218) And shortly afterwards she says to herself that 'the whole of my family's honour lies in my sacrifice.' (Vol 1 p 226) Here again she uses the Sanskrit and Hindi word *balidan*. When her family lose track of her in the upheavals and presume she has been killed, her brother Puri says of her, 'Tara has become a sacrifice.' (Vol 1 p 425) He uses another common word of Sanskrit origin, *ahuti*.

This sort of sacrificial language is developed more powerfully in the context of Shashi's marriage in *Shekhar a Life* when Shekhar reflects that 'a wife's soul is always a sacrificed soul (hutatma)'. (Vol 2 p 69) Again, the first three letters of this word are derived from the same Sanskrit word as *ahuti*. This is quite a common expression[10] and says something profound about the traditional Hindu view of women. In these two novels it seems that kind of language is deliberately used in extreme situations in order to criticise it. Ajneya and Yashpal imply that if sacrifice demands such terrible suffering of women then the very concept needs to be questioned – and therefore the traditional role of women put in question as well. This point is endorsed by Shekhar who says that Shashi is continually sacrificing herself for his sake, but that he cannot accept this sacrifice. (Vol 2 p 218) So in the experience of both Shashi and Tara we find a transmutation of the language of sacrifice, and so of the victim, which becomes part of the struggle to find a new relationship between women and men.

The language of sacrifice is used in other contexts as well. According to Yashpal one of the chief marks of the new India, and indeed of the old, is corruption. In such an environment those who try to keep their integrity always run the risk of losing their jobs. Early in the first volume of this two volume work Jaydeva Puri, Tara's brother, is working for a newspaper in Lahore as tension mounts between Hindus and Muslims. After the death of Daulu Mama he writes an even-handed editorial in which he speaks out against the communal violence perpetrated by both sides, and as a result loses his job, because the Hindu proprietor is afraid of what will happen to his paper's circulation. So Puri becomes the victim of his own integrity.

But the real heroine of the second volume of the novel

---

[10]I was informed of this by Dr. Satyendra Srivastava, Lecturer in Hindi, Cambridge University, in a conversation in 1991.

as of the first is Tara. After her terrible experiences during
Partition she arrives in Delhi and after many struggles and
disappointments eventually gets a good job with the government in the new India. Her new life cannot be compared
to the nightmare which came before it, but it is still a life
which the language of suffering and sacrifice is particularly apt to describe. She refuses to give or take bribes.
She supports the demands of the Unions to give better
working conditions with proper time off to domestic servants, and this brings down on her head the wrath of her
prosperous neighbours who see their own servants as get-
ting ambitions beyond their proper status as a result.

At an earlier point, when she is at the nadir of her
fortunes in Lahore, she finds herself in the company of
some simple village women who have suffered as much as
she has. They still believe in God and the gods but Tara
cannot share their faith. Like Shekhar, she finds that all
the old sources of meaning have collapsed. One night she
cannot sleep and the events of her past life come into her
mind. She reflects to herself:

> Was she born only to suffer trouble ? Why had she
> been born into a poor household ? Why can she not
> find peace of mind by believing that her poverty is the
> fruit of previous births ? Why does she want freedom
> from poverty ? How did she get the thought of marry-
> ing according to her own choice ? Why can't she ac-
> cept life with all its pleasures and pains like Shilo [a
> simple and uneducated relative] ? That terrible [wed-
> ding] night at her in-laws ! The deceitful love of the
> Muslims ! [who only wanted to convert her.] But
> what would have been the harm in becoming a Mus-
> lim ? Why had she refused the suggestion ? What had
> her Hinduness given to her ? What help had it given

> her? Her women companions still held on to their
> Hinduness, what does the future hold?(Vol 1 p 457)

Yet although at that moment Tara cannot find it in her, as
Shekhar had struggled to do, to tell her own story in a way
that can give her life any kind of meaning,Yashpal as the
author is telling her story for her throughout the whole
novel.

These points need to be set in a more general context:
the victim's story needs to be heard, and more than simply
heard, it needs also to be remembered, even if the story
makes no sense to the victim and indeed even if the victim,
like Tara, cannot discern any story at all, but only a suc-
cession of meaningless and horrific events. That need for
remembering is a profound theme of much Jewish writing
about the Holocaust. People who survived the horrors of
the Nazi death camps feel bound to tell the story of what
happened in them, not only for the sake of those who did
not survive, but so that the rest of us can never forget what
happened.[11] But though important, it is not enough for the
Jews to tell their story. If remembering is to be complete
then that story has to be included in the larger story of
those who shared responsibility for the suffering in the
first place. Thus European Christians face the challenge of
retelling the story of our own history in a way which
acknowledges and includes the long and shameful history
of Christian anti-Semitism. That has profound implications
for the way we perceive our own identity.

In Britain too our predominantly white churches also
face the task of listening to and then including in our own

---

[11]See, for example, Primo Levi, *If This Is a Man* and *The
Truce*, Abacus, London, 1987, and Elie Wiesel, *Night*, Penguin Books, London, 1981.

story the stories of the many black Christians who now live
among us. When I was a boy at school I learnt much about
how William Wilberforce and others had fought for the
abolition of the slave trade. I learnt little or nothing of the
way in which the wealth of cities such as Bristol and
Liverpool had been built on the foundation of that trade.
We have to re-visit and re-member our past if the future is
to be more hopeful.

To return to our novels: there are some important
reflections on the nature and role of victims in *Shekhar a
Life*. There is a depth and quality about these which are not
to be found in Yashpal's novel. In the previous chapter I
described how Shekhar was expelled from the Brahmin
students' hostel at the college in Madras because he re-
fused to keep to the purity regulations surrounding food
and eating. After his expulsion he goes to live in the scheduled caste students' hostel. He also sets up a small school
for poor children in a slum area of the city. An open drain
flows through this little colony and one evening Shekhar is
standing beside it:

> The water of the drain was gleaming like old copper.
> If there had not been a bad smell it would have been
> difficult at that moment to say that the water was
> dirty. As he was thinking, it was as if a wall fell
> before his concentrated strength and a path began to
> appear. He remembered from the Bible the story of
> John the Baptist, the forerunner of Jesus. It was in a
> place like this that the young man must have stood —
> with frenzied eyes, scattered untidy hair and wiry
> body, wearing a deer-skin. He cried, 'Come ! I will
> anoint you with the water of life'. And it was on just
> such a dirty red evening that the people of low caste,
> the rejected dregs of humanity, rejected what he said,

saying that he must be mad; but hearing his continuous crying out they came to see what the water of life was.

It seemed to Shekhar entirely appropriate that he should remember that on this spot, for what is the water of life ? The water of the Ganges, Jamuna, Godavari, Krishna and Narmada has become lifeless through continuous washing in *dharma* and *bhakti*. If life, eternal life is to be found anywhere it is only in such filthy drains which flow, long neglected, in the midst of these untouchables who are the foundation of society...the water of the so-called holy rivers which fall from heaven is over-flowing like the knowledge of the pundits, its only use is to be sprinkled on funeral pyres and to carry away bones in its onward flowing stream. (Vol 1 p 215)

Shekhar's reflections on the baptism of Jesus enable him to stand with the victims in his imagination and to discern in them a profound human dignity, to the point that he begins to see in them, the rejected and outcast, the very foundation of the society which rejects them. That is implicit in the stories of victims which he recounts later in the novel and which we have already discussed.

This theme is taken up in a rather different way when he moves to Lahore at the beginning of the second volume. That is where Shashi and her family live and it is here that he meets with her again after an interval of many years. It is at this time that Shashi's father dies and he goes to offer his condolences to the family. He says to Shashi, 'The shadow of pain is a kind of tapasya, by means of it the soul is purified.' Now *tapasya* is an important word which in the Hindu tradition normally refers to the voluntary austerities which people undertake in order to purify their souls.

But Shashi rebukes Shekhar and replies, 'Pain purifies the soul of the one who tries to remove it, no-one else's'. (Vol 2 p 33) She thanks him for coming to share her pain but then rebukes him for wanting to rest in its shadow and says to him, 'Pain is everywhere'. For her there is an inescapable link between the active attempt to remove the suffering of others and the inner purification to which Shekhar wants to lay claim. She makes no appeal to traditional interpretations of suffering and would no doubt have agreed with Madansingh to whom I referred above. He was the long term political prisoner whom Shekhar was later to meet in jail. He argued that the Indian tradition has been too inward-looking and individualist in its attitude with the result that the quest for salvation tends to separate the seeker from society.

The memory of Shashi's rebuke leads Shekhar to make an apparently unimportant decision which is to have fateful consequences. After her father's funeral he returns to college in Lahore and along with many other students enrols as a volunteer to help in the administration of the session of the National Congress Party which is to be held in a large tented encampment. He is given a position of authority over the other volunteers and one night he makes a tour of the sentries. He finds one man un-complainingly beginning his third consecutive stint – his two replacements having failed to run up. Remembering Shashi's words about removing the pain of other Shekhar takes this man's place. While he is standing there he is arrested by the police on a false charge. As he is being driven away in the police car he thinks again of Shashi's words, 'Pain only purifies the soul of the one who tries to remove it'. He then adds his own gloss to her words, 'Purification is to be found not in suffering with another, but in suffering in their place.' (Vol 2 p 43) Later on, when he is actually in jail, we find him reflecting on the significance of the death of Christ:

> Is it this which is the doctrine of substitutionary sacri-
> fice which he had read somewhere in a book and
> rejected as unacceptable — that our pain can be the
> atonement for someone else's sin ? Is every person the
> Jesus Christ of someone else ? Is this the first and last
> gleam of light in this hell of torment ?(Vol 2 p 80)

So here Shekhar has moved beyond merely listening to the
victim's story to a deliberate decision to take the victim's
place. And he turns to the Christian faith as a way of
interpreting what he has done. It is tempting to claim that
Ajneya at this point is deeply influenced by the Christian
faith. That may indeed be true. I think it is more appropriate for me to suggest that he is using Christianity to en-
dorse conclusions he may have already reached on other
grounds through his use of the language of Hindu sacrifice.
That may equally well be true. In that case we can perhaps
talk of a convergence of Ajneya's thought with certain
Christian insights. As a further antidote to instinctive
Christian triumphalism I have already argued that Christians have plenty of work to do in putting their own house
in order. But just as a novel can take on new meanings in
new contexts, so too can the Christian story — and indeed
the Hindu and Muslim stories too. One key to those new
meanings, I have suggested, is to be found in the stories of
the victims, whoever the victims may be.

I have argued in these three chapters that novels
offer us a fruitful way into making sense of our plural
world. They enable us to over-hear conversations which
are already going on and so offer a new depth and complexity to inter-faith conversation and dialogue. Perhaps
most importantly, they raise many of the questions about
religion which religious people also need to ask for them-

selves but do not always see or perhaps want to see. In telling the stories of the victims *Shekhar: a Life* and *A False Truth* implicitly suggest ways in which we can all include such stories within our own larger story. But our own story has to be modified in the process, and in this way the victims challenge us to reshape our accounts of our own identity. Here is a strategy of resistance to the language of arrogant, blind, and unitary exclusivism which is so vociferous and powerful today within all religious communities. Those who are imprisoned in that kind of language see their identity as fixed and unalterable, yet that can never be so, for all identities are subject to continual renegotiation, and the stories which enshrine them have continually to be reshaped and retold. The three novels which I have examined in these chapters are illustrations of the way in which novels and novelists can be our allies in this struggle. Can we today narrate the nation — whatever our nation may be — in any other way?